CHART TOPPER

IMP's Top 20 Best Selling POP HITS

CONTENTS

Exclusive distributors:
International Music Publications Limited: Southend Road, Woodford Green, Essex IG8 8HN
International Music Publications GmbH Germany: Marstallstrasse 8, D-80539 München, Germany
Nuova Carisch S.p.a. - Italy: Via Campania 12, 20098 San Guiliano Milanese, Milano, Italy
Nuova Carisch S.p.a. - France: 25 rue d'hauteville, 75010 Paris, France
Nuova Carisch S.p.a. - Spain: Magallenes 25, 28015 Madrid, Spain
Danmusik: Vognmagergade 7, DK-1120 Copenhagen K, Denmark

Production: Miranda Steel

Published 1998

© International Music Publications Limited
Southend Road, Woodford Green, Essex IG8 8HN, England

2

Angels

Words and Music by
ROBBIE WILLIAMS and **GUY CHAMBERS**

3

Bohemian Rhapsody

Words and Music by
FREDDIE MERCURY

12

14

Baby Can I Hold You Tonight

Words and Music by
TRACY CHAPMAN

Flashdance... What A Feeling

Words by IRENE CARA and KEITH FORSEY
Music by GIORGIO MORODER

20

Hotel California

Words and Music by
DON HENLEY, GLENN FREY and **DON FELDER**

Moderate Rock beat

On a dark des-ert high - way,
Her mind is Tif - fa - ny twist - ed.

cool wind in my
She got the Mer - ce - des

29

Frozen

Words and Music by
MADONNA CICCONE and **PATRICK LEONARD**

32

How Do I Live

Words and Music by
DIANE WARREN

Moderately slow ♩ = 92

1. How do I _____ get through one night with-out___ you.___ If I had to
2. *See additional lyrics*

live with-out___ you,___ what kind of life would that be?___ Oh,___ I,_____ I need you in my

arms, need you___ to hold.___ You're my world, my heart,___ my soul. If you ev-er leave,___

EMI Music Publishing Ltd, London WC2H 0EA

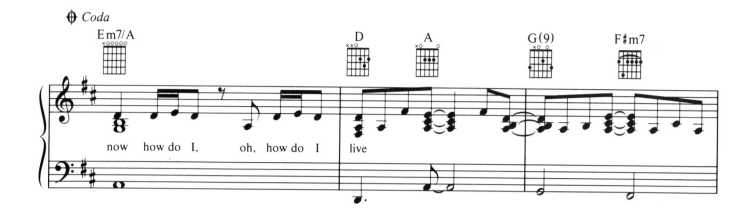

now how do I, oh, how do I live

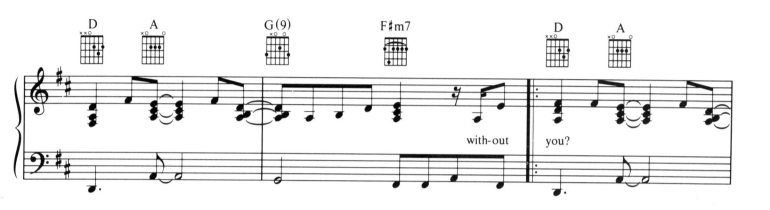

with-out you?

Repeat ad lib. and fade
(vocal 1st time only)

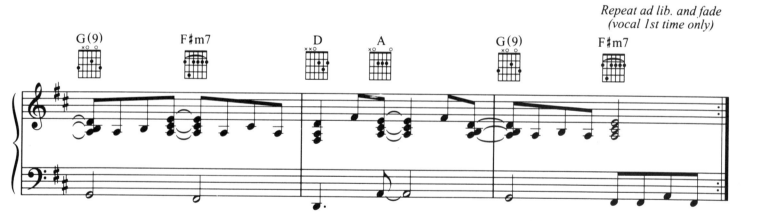

Verse 2:
Without you, there'd be no sun in my sky,
There would be no love in my life,
There'd be no world left for me.
And I, baby, I don't know what I would do,
I'd be lost if I lost you.
If you ever leave,
Baby, you would take away everything real in my life.
And tell me now...
(To Chorus:)

I'll Be There For You

Words and Music by
**PHIL SOLEM, MARTA KAUFFMAN, DAVID CRANE,
MICHAEL SKLOFF, ALLEE WILLIS and DANNY WILDE**

* Guitar fill reads 8va.

er know — me, no one could ev - er see — me.

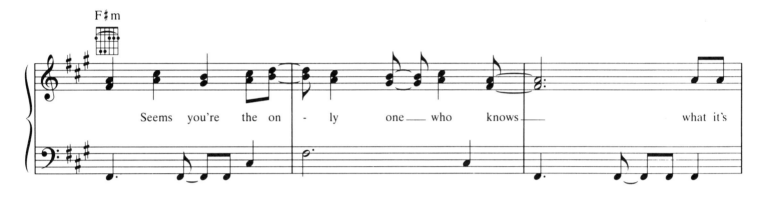

Seems you're the on - ly one — who knows — what it's

like to be — me. Some - one to face — the day — with,

make it through all — the rest — with, some - one I'll al -

Kiss The Rain

Words and Music by
BILLIE MYERS, DESMOND CHILD and ERIC BAZILIAN

50

Verse 2:
Hello? Do you miss me?
I hear you say you do,
But not the way I'm missing you.
What's new? How's the weather?
Is it stormy where you are?
You sound so close,
But it feels like you're so far.
Oh, would it mean anything
If you knew what I'm left imagining
In my mind, in my mind.
Would you go, would you go...
(To Chorus:)

Lady Marmalade

Words and Music by
BOB CREWE and KENNY NOLAN

Hey sis - ter, go sis - ter, soul sis - ter, go sis - ter.

Verse 1: (spoken)

Do you fancy enough, hit him in the sack
Yes my kitty cat is a wreck
And then some, you are the one
Gotta represent, gotta go the whole run.
We can play all night, gotta do it right
Snuggle up, huddle up, nice and tight
My place or yours, gotta be raw
Don't really matter once we get through the door.

Verse 3: (spoken)

Mocca chocolata ha
Coucher ce soir
Run, run that's right
Bring it on daddy it's the bedroom fight.
Get ahead, get your drawers and put them on fast
Got to keep up if you think you can last
Gonna get wet, are you ready yet?
On your marks, get set.

Let Me Entertain You

Words and Music by
ROBBIE WILLIAMS and **GUY CHAMBERS**

Hell is gone and hea-ven's here, there's no-thing left_ for you to fear,___ shake your arse come ov-er here, now scream. I'm a burn-ing ef-fi-gy_ of ev-ery-thing I used to be you're my rock of em-pa-thy, my dear. So come on

Life's too short for you to die so grab your-self an a-li-bi hea-ven knows your mo-ther lied, mon cher. Se-pa-rate your right from wrongs, come and sing a dif-ferent song, the ket-tle's on so don't be long, mon cher. So come on

My Heart Will Go On

Words by WILL JENNINGS
Music by JAMES HORNER

64

Stand By Me

Words and Music by
JERRY LEIBER, MIKE STOLLER and **BEN E KING**

74

Promise Me

Words and Music by
BEVERLEY CRAVEN

And I'll be_ home, I'll be_ home_ soon.

I'll be_ home_

soon.

Something About The Way You Look Tonight

Words by BERNIE TAUPIN
Music by ELTON JOHN

There was a time I was ev-ery-thing and no-thing all in one.

When you found me I was feel-ing like a cloud a-cross the sun.

Stairway To Heaven

Words and Music by
JIMMY PAGE and ROBERT PLANT

Tomorrow Never Dies

Words and Music by
SHERYL CROW and MITCHELL FROOM

Verse 2:
Darling, you've won; it's no fun,
Martinis, girls and guns.
It's murder on our love affair,
But you bet your life, every night
While you're chasing the morning light,
You're not the only spy out there.
It's so deadly, my dear,
The power of wanting you near.
(To Chorus:)

Say You Love Me

Words and Music by
MICK HUCKNALL

X-Files

By MARK SNOW

Moderately ♩ = 96

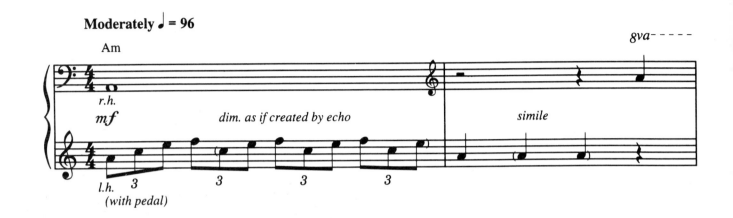

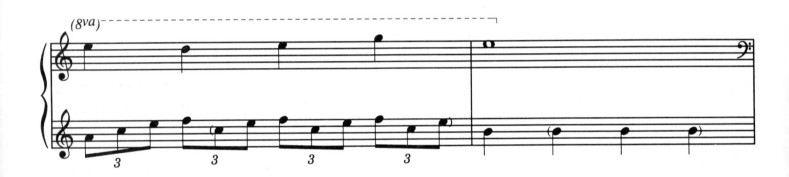

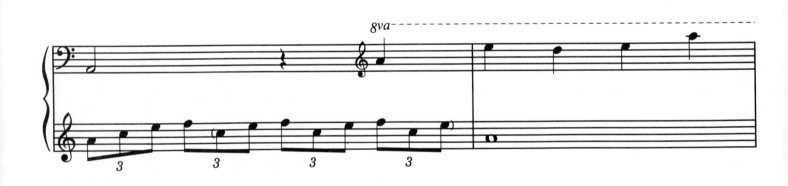

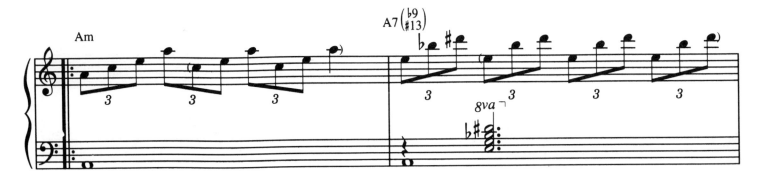

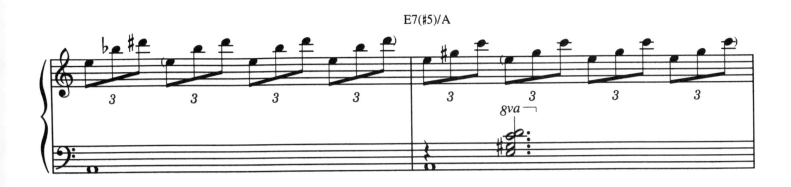

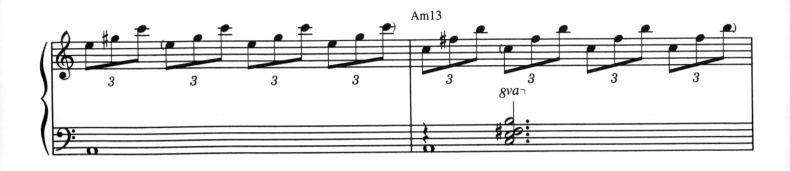

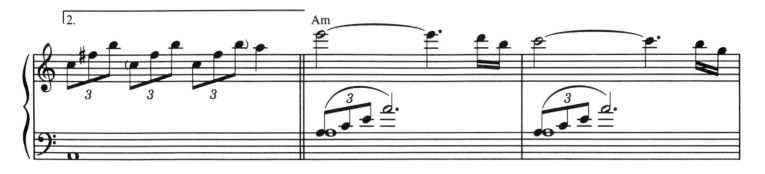

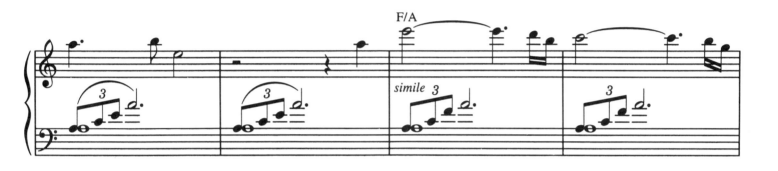

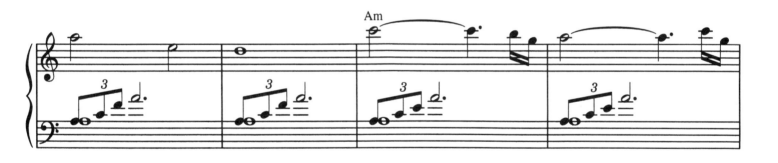

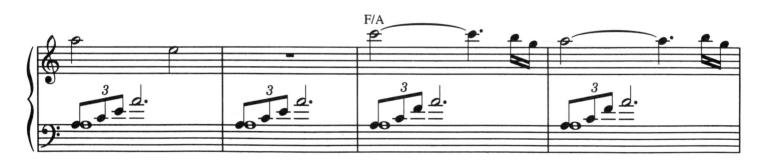

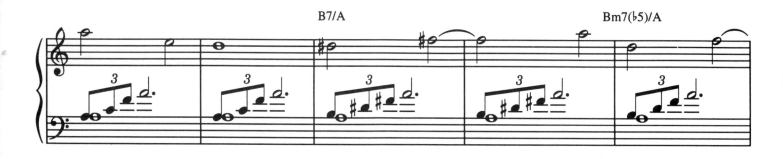

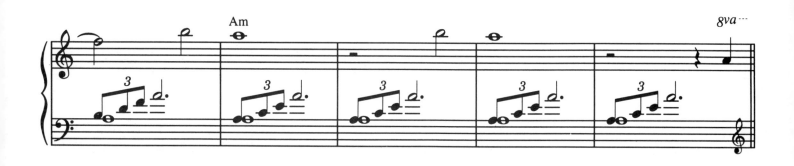

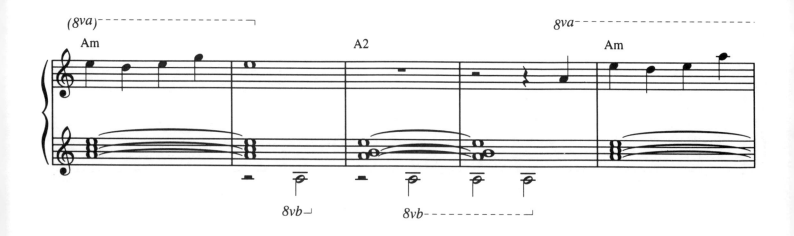

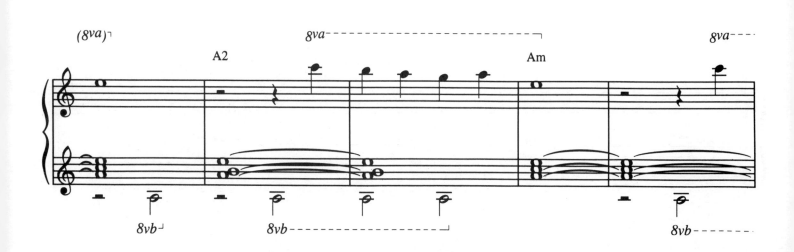

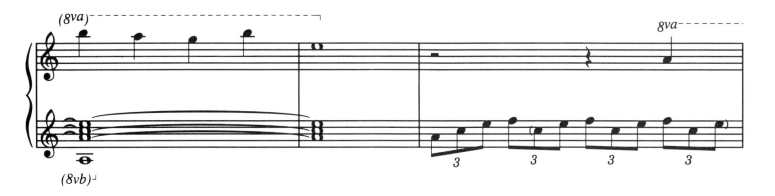

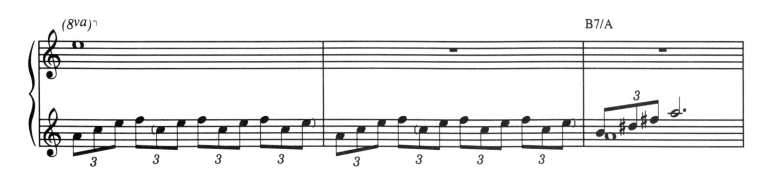

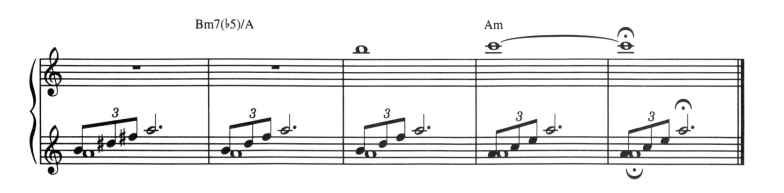

You Sexy Thing

Words and Music by
ERROL BROWN

Printed in England
The Panda Group · Haverhill · Suffolk · 10/98

Other hits collections available

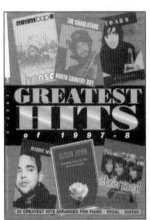

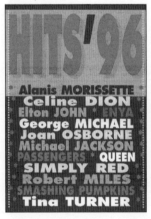